the

CW00497207

travel

websites

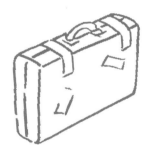

Zingin.com

An Imprint of Pearson Education

London New York Toronto Sydney Tokyo
Singapore Madrid Mexico City Munich Paris

PEARSON EDUCATION LIMITED

Head Office:
Edinburgh Gate
Harlow CM20 2JE
Tel: +44 (0)1279 623623
Fax: +44 (0)1279 431059

London Office:
128 Long Acre
London WC2E 9AN
Tel: +44 (0)20 7447 2000
Fax: +44 (0)20 7240 5771

First published in Great Britain in 2000

© Paul Carr 2000

ISBN 0-130-40939-1

British Library Cataloguing-in-Publication Data
A catalogue record for this book can be obtained from the British Library.

10 9 8 7 6 5 4 3 2 1

Typeset by Land & Unwin (Data Sciences) Ltd
Printed and bound by Ashford Colour Press, Gosport, Hampshire

The publisher's policy is to use paper manufactured from sustainable forests.

contents

While the publisher and author have made every effort to ensure that all entries were correct when this book went to press, the Internet moves so quickly that there may now be website addresses that don't work, or new sites we should cover. If you encounter any incorrect entries when using the book, please send us an email at **oops@zingin.com** *and we will make sure it is dealt with in the next edition.*

The publisher and author can accept no responsibility for any loss or inconvenience sustained by the reader as a result of the content of this book.

A family holiday in the sun ... a voyage of discovery to India ... a business trip to Brussels. Going away just got a whole lot easier.

Travel has become one of the most popular uses of the internet and a huge number of sites have sprung up in the past couple of years to meet the growing demand for low-cost holidays, flights, accommodation and just about everything else. The difficult part is knowing which ones are worthy of your attention and which are just a waste of web space.

If you've ever tried to make travel arrangements online you'll know just how much choice there is out there – imagine a million travel brochures, train timetables and guide books with no index or indication of where to start. Far from making life easier, the sheer information overload is enough to make even the most dedicated net-head run screaming for the nearest high street travel agent.

When we originally launched Zingin.com the plan was to create a user-friendly, UK-focused guide to the best of the web. Although the site itself has grown rapidly since those early days, we're still very choosy about which sites we recommend to our users.

With this in mind, when we decided to put this book together we were determined not to create just another huge list of travel sites – there's enough of them around and they just add to the confusion. Instead, we've tried to provide a user-friendly guide to the best of the internet travel bunch. From travel agents to tourist advice, road maps to rough guides and everything in between – if it's useful and relevant, you'll find it here – if it's not, you won't.

So who is the book written for? Well, if you're a UK user who wants to get straight to the best internet travel resources then it's for you! Family holidaymakers, backpackers, business travellers, campers, skiers, surfers and commuters – no matter where you're going, we'll point you in the right direction.

We've tried to make it as easy as possible for you just to dive in and get started with the book. The chapters have been put in a (hopefully) logical order, starting with sites that help you to arrange your journey, then those that suggest things to do – and not to do – when you get there and finally all of the extra bits and pieces you might need along the way.

Although only the very best of the web has made it into these pages, we've headed up each section with **the best of the best** so you don't have to waste any time getting started, and if you know the name of the site you want, you can look it up in the quick reference section tucked away neatly at the back.

With the help of this book it should be pretty straightforward to find the information you're looking for but if you do have any problems please come and visit us on the web (**www.zingin.com**) and we'll try our best to help you out.

Bon voyage!

Paul Carr
Founder
Zingin.com

the internet:
a (very) brief guide

The fact that you've bought this book means that you've probably used the internet before, either at home or at work. If, however, you're still getting to grips with the basics then read on for the answers to some of our most frequently asked questions.

Getting started

There are plenty of online resources to help you get the most out of the web but none of them are any use if you're not online. By far the quickest way to get started is to pop into your local newsagent or computer shop and get hold of one of the zillions of free internet access CDs stuck to the front of popular computer magazines. However, if you want a bit more information before taking the plunge have a quick look at the following pointers.

I'm new to the internet, how do I get started?

It goes without saying that to take advantage of the information contained in this book, you'll need access to the internet. If you want to connect from home you'll need a computer (a 486 or above should be fine), a modem (new computers usually come with one built in) and a spare telephone socket within easy reach of the computer.

The modem, which plugs in to the back of your computer (unless it's already built in) and then into the telephone socket, has basically one purpose – to allow your computer to send and receive data over a telephone line. Once you're plugged in, all that remains now is to decide which internet service provider (ISP) you will use to connect to the 'net. Your ISP provides a gateway to the internet and when you ask your computer to connect to the web or to send and receive e-mails, your modem is actually dialling into their network which, in turn, is connected to the rest of the internet. This explains how you can send an e-mail to Egypt or to Edinburgh for the same price – you're only paying for the call to the ISP (the price of a local call or less). If you don't want to connect from home then most large libraries provide free or low-cost internet access and there are plenty of internet cafés around the country who will be happy to help you take your first online steps.

Which ISP is right for me?

Choosing an ISP can be a complicated business with some companies offering free access, some offering free telephone calls and a few still clinging on to monthly charges – all trying to persuade you that you'll get a better deal with them. Pretty confusing. Basically, the right ISP for you will depend on what you want to use the internet for.

If you're only interested in e-mail, surfing the web and maybe building a personal website then you'll be fine with a free service. Of course, there's no such thing as a free lunch and you'll usually still have to pay either local call charges or a fixed fee for unlimited access. Luckily for internet users, there's fierce competition between ISPs and you can find some excellent deals if you shop around. To get online with a free service you can either pick up a connection CD from one of the high street shops who have set up their own ISPs (WHSmiths, PC World, Waterstones and Tesco to name just a few) or call up one of the providers advertised in any of the popular internet magazines.

If you want to use the internet for business and require extra features such as high speed access, a business website or your own domain name (e.g. you@yourname.com) then you'll need use a specialist ISP who will usually charge a monthly fee in addition to your normal phone charges.

If you already have internet access at work, university, school or in a local internet café then surf over to ISP Review (www.ispreview.co.uk) for a full run-down of the best and worst UK internet service providers.

Online help and advice

Ok, so you've made it online and you're looking for help and advice on how to get the most out of the web? Of course, to find the best websites to get you started you'll want to take a quick trip to your friends at Zingin.com (**www.zingin.com**) but for technical support and general advice, try these.

Why does it say that the page I'm looking for is not found?

The internet is in a constant state of development and things are getting moved around and deleted all the time. Anyone who's spent more than a couple of minutes on the web will have clicked on a link or typed in a web address only to get hit with the dreaded 'File not found' message. If the page you're looking for seems to have vanished, the most likely cause is that the page has been deleted or moved to another address. If an address doesn't work, try removing bits from the end until you find something. For example; if the address **www.asite.com/directory/files/filename.html** produces an error, try deleting the 'filename.html' bit to see if there's anything at **www.asite.com/directory/files**. If you're still getting an error then try **www.asite.com/directory** and finally **www.asite.com**. If you run out of things to delete and still can't find the site then it's probably temporarily unavailable or has been deleted. Sites that have been moved can often be tracked down using a search engine such as Google (**www.google.com**) – simply type in the name of the page/site and see what comes up.

What is the best software for browsing the web?

Most of the free ISPs include a copy of Microsoft Internet Explorer on their access disks and, unless you really want to, there's no real need to use another browser. If you do fancy a change or want to fight back against Microsoft's quest for world domination, there are some alternatives worth trying. The best of the bunch is Netscape Navigator which contains a very similar range of features to Internet Explorer but with slightly less polish. The best way to describe Netscape is like Burger King to Microsoft's McDonald's – try them both and decide which one tastes better. Other choices can be found at **www.browserwatch.com**.

How can I find out more about using the web?

The internet used to be controlled by academics, scientists and computer geeks and unless you knew your way around it could be very scary indeed. In cyberspace no one could hear you scream. Nowadays, using e-mail and surfing the web is like driving a car – pretty straightforward when you get the hang of it even if you don't know exactly what's going on under the bonnet. Having said that, if you want to get the most out of your internet experience you'll need to get a basic grasp of the way it works. One of the best guides to how the 'net works and what it can do is Learn the Net (**www.learnthenet.com**) which contains some very well-written tutorials covering e-mail, downloading files, building a website and plenty of other useful stuff. If you're baffled by internet jargon you'll definitely want to have a quick look at PC Webopedia (**www.pcwebopedia.com**) and for beginner's advice with a UK perspective surf over to BBC Webwise (**www.bbc.co.uk/ webwise**).

Buying online

Throughout this book you'll find sites that allow you to order products, book tickets and generally spend your hard-earned cash. The first thing to remember is that using your credit card online is 100% safe providing you take a few sensible precautions.

How do I know which companies to trust?

Firstly, wherever possible stick to companies you've heard of. If someone you know has bought from a particular site without any problems or if it's a household name then the risk is greatly reduced.

As with any purchase on or off the web, you should always ensure that you are buying from a reputable company. Sites such as Amazon (**www.amazon.co.uk**) and Last Minute (**www.lastminute.com**) are very well-known internet traders and so are a risk-free option but if you do want to order from a company you've never heard of then take a look at the next few questions which will hopefully address your concerns.

Can hackers get hold of my credit card number once I've typed it in?

As long as you only type your credit card details into sites that offer encryption security (SSL), your information will be perfectly safe. Look for a yellow padlock on the bottom right of your browser window if you are using Internet Explorer or, in Netscape, look for a closed padlock. This ensures that information sent to the site is encrypted and so cannot be intercepted by hackers. If the site is not secure, be very wary about placing an online order and *never* send credit card information via normal e-mail.

How can I check on the status of my order?

Many larger sites offer order tracking facilities which allow you to check the progress of your order until it is delivered. If there is no order tracking, ensure there is a contact telephone number in case you need to chase things up.

Is it safe to order from outside the UK?

Orders placed with companies outside the UK are not protected by UK sale of goods or safety legislation. Only order from abroad if you know and trust the company you are dealing with and even then, try to stick within Western Europe and the USA.

Am I going to get stung by hidden costs?

There's no 'internet tax' for orders made online but as with any mail order purchase you should always check whether your order includes postage and packing costs. Also, remember that orders from outside the UK may be subject to additional customs and import costs.

Is there a regulatory body for online traders?

The Consumers Association have been looking after the interests of shoppers for years and have recently launched a scheme to protect you on the web. The Which? Webtrader scheme (**www.which.net/webtrader**) requires its members to abide by a strict code of conduct if they want to join. Sites that have the Webtrader logo have to provide a decent level of service otherwise Which? will simply kick them out! It's worth remembering that membership of the scheme isn't compulsory and many reputable businesses are not members, so if you don't see the logo don't assume the worst, but if you do – expect the best.

What if the goods don't arrive or my credit card is used fraudulently?

Don't panic if products ordered online take a while to arrive. Just like in the real world, delays do happen and things can be out of stock – even if you receive a confirmation saying that everything is fine. However, if you've waited longer than 21 days then you should contact the company concerned to hurry them up.

A gentle reminder will usually be enough to get things moving but if you're still not getting anywhere you should contact your credit card issuer for advice. If the site is a member of the Which? Webtrader scheme, make sure you let them know as well.

If you have problems with an order made using a credit card, you will usually be able to recover any lost money from your card issuer. If you're concerned about fraud, call your credit card company to check their policy regarding fraudulent transactions.

Can I buy anything I like over the web?

Yes and no. Yes, most things are available – from sweets and cakes to cars and houses but, no, you can't necessarily order them from the UK. The law on ordering from abroad using the internet is the same as using the phone and there are certain products which it is illegal to bring into the country. Some good examples of this are: drugs, certain food items, adult material, pets and automatic weapons. You can probably guess the law's position on drugs and guns but if you need to check out what is allowed, visit Customs and Excise (**www.hmce.gov.uk**).

For the full low-down on internet Shopping, check out the Zingin's *The very best shopping websites.*

Searching the web

Finding what you're looking for on the internet can be like trying to find a very small needle in a very large haystack. Search engines are fine if you're looking for very specialist information (the population of Peru or the Belgian translation of *Romeo and Juliet*) but when it comes to popular subjects like travel or music it's easy to get swamped by the number of sites available.

So how do you find the information you need without wading through pages of irrelevant junk? Good question.

What is the best search engine?

That all depends on what you're looking for. There are literally thousands of search engines and directory sites and each has its own strengths and weaknesses.

For general searches we recommend Google (www.google.com) which ranks sites on both relevance and popularity (how many other sites link to them). You'll usually find the information you want on the first page of results but if you have no success, try the same search on Hotbot (www.hotbot.com) and Altavista (www.altavista.co.uk)

If you are looking for UK-specific information there are plenty of home-grown search engines which should fit the bill. A couple of our favourites are UK Plus (www.ukplus.co.uk) and Search UK (www.searchuk.co.uk).

How do I find a business or service?

Looking for a plumber? An electrician? A four-star hotel in Derby? Rather than reaching for the *Yellow Pages*, take a wander over to Scoot (**www.scoot.co.uk**) which will let you search by business type, location or the name of the company you need. If you prefer to use good old *Yellow Pages* then it can be found at Yell (**www.yell.com**).

Is it really possible to get free software over the internet? Where can I find it?

The internet is full of free software, much of which can be downloaded for just the price of a telephone call. Generally, unless you are willing to spend some money, you will only be able to get a trial version of the program which will stop working after a short period of time (usually 30 days). If you want to carry on using it after that you'll have to pay for it – often at a substantial discount over the normal retail price. To get your hands on the best of the freebies, try searching Download.com (**www.download.com**) and Tucows (**www.tucows.com**).

Where can I find the best online shops?

As the number of internet traders has increased, so have the directories that promise to tell you where to find them. One of the most popular shopping directories is Shopsmart (**www.shopsmart.com**) but our personal favourite is 2020 Shops (**www.2020shops.com**) which provides friendly reviews of each of the stores and a useful rating system to help you get started. If you want to compare prices before you buy, you can shop around quickly and easily with the excellent Hoojit (**www.hoojit.com**) or Kelkoo (**uk.kelkoo.com**).

So many search engines, so little time – is there an alternative?

Funny you should ask! You can access the search engines listed above directly from The Zingin Search Guide (www.zingin.com/ guide/search) and there's a complete listing of UK and global search tools in our Information Guide (www.zingin.com/guide/ info/search).

2

getting there

Portals and travel agents

Making your travel plans online need not be any more stressful than, say, buying a book or a CD. Once you've decided where you want to go you simply find a travel agent, fill in a few boxes and you're off! Ok ... it's not *quite* that simple – travel is an expensive business and there are a zillion travel companies out there, each offering different packages, prices and options.

No matter what type of journey you're planning, your first stop should be one of the popular online travel agents or portal sites which will either allow you to book tickets directly or at least point you in the right direction.

If you're concerned about booking a holiday with a company you've never heard of, it's worth bearing in mind that the vast majority of internet travel sites are actually operated by long-established high street names. Provided you stick with our suggested sites, making travel bookings online should be a risk-free affair but, for added peace of mind, you can make sure your chosen agent is a member of ABTA by visiting **www.abtanet.com**.

So, you want to book a holiday but don't know where to start? Here's our list of recommended sites.

■ The best of the best

A2B Travel **www.a2btravel.co.uk**

No matter where, how or why you're travelling, don't leave home until you've checked out A2B Travel. A2B is the UK's largest travel information and booking portal. As it's designed by publishing giant EMAP, you'd expect excellent design and content but even by their normal standards this is something special. The layout may be a little cluttered for some tastes but it only reinforces how much information is packed into the site. Whether you prefer to travel by plane, train or Eurostar you'll find timetables, online booking and everything else you might need.

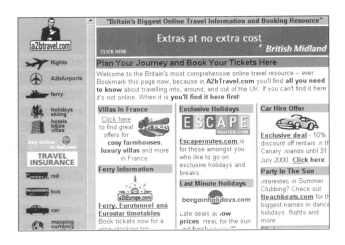

A2B have also put together a network of specialist sites which are designed to make your journey that little bit smoother. Check out A2B Airports (www.a2bairports.com), Escape Routes (www.escaperoutes.net) and A2B Europe (www.a2beurope.com) for starters.

■ The rest of the best

Travelocity www.travelocity.co.uk

While Travelocity does offer plenty of useful travel information, including some well-written destination guides, the site's main strength is its easy-to-use flight and hotel booking system. Behind the wonderfully cluttered front page you'll find a veritable goldmine of flights, hotel rooms, package holidays, weekend breaks and car hire. Tread carefully though, the prices offered are not always the cheapest available so it's worth checking Expedia (www.expedia.co.uk), Teletext (www.teletext.co.uk/holidays) and the rest to make sure you're getting the best deal.

Expedia www.expedia.co.uk

The formula here is the same as the other travel sites with flights, accommodation and car hire but the real prize-winner is their price comparison tool which lets you find the best deal on your holiday.

Thomas Cook www.thomascook.co.uk

Not quite as impressive as some of the internet-only travel agents but the high street giant does offer a wide range of package holidays which will particularly appeal to family holidaymakers. Definitely worth a look for off-season travel.

Utravel www.utravel.co.uk

Utravel may be a relative newcomer to the online travel arena but it's quickly become a thoroughly decent alternative to the more established sites. Rather than focusing on one specific area of travel, you'll find everything from flights to ferries covered in more than acceptable detail. Admittedly most of the stuff here is done better by A2B but, as wannabes go, it's one of the best.

QXL Travel Auctions www.qxl.com

Proof that making travel plans can be exciting, QXL allows you to bid against other holidaymakers for a wide range of flights and packages. Reserve prices are generally quite low but QXL is a very busy site so expect the bidding to be fierce. Depending on how desirable the holiday is you may not make much of a saving by buying this way but you certainly can't beat the sense of achievement when you do.

Teletext www.teletext.co.uk/holidays

Teletext's holiday site offers some of the UK's lowest holiday prices – and you won't need to hunt for the remote control to find them.

Bargain Holidays www.bargainholidays.com

Fun in the sun without breaking the bank.

Brochure Bank www.brochurebank.co.uk

Save yourself the hassle of traipsing around travel agents. These folk will deliver brochures from the UK's leading tour operators direct to your door – free of charge.

■ The best of the rest

Air Miles www.airmiles.co.uk
Travel, collect points, then travel some more. You know the drill.

Airtours www.airtours.com
Nice-looking site from one of the UK's largest holiday companies.

Butlins www.butlins.co.uk
Hi-de-hi campers. Suitably bright and cheerful site from this British institution.

Center Parcs www.centerparcs.co.uk
Relax and recharge your batteries in a big bubble of holiday fun.

Co-op Travelcare www.co-op-travelcare.co.uk
Cheap flights, cheap holidays, cheap everything. Nice site though.

Express Flight www.expressflight.com
Specialising in providing flights at wholesale prices. Bargains galore!

Holiday Discounts www.holidaydiscounts.com
Looking for a discount holiday? No more clues.

High street favourites
If you can't bear to put your faith in an internet-only travel agent:

| Lunn Poly | www.lunn-poly.com |
| Thomson Holidays | www.thomson-holidays.co.uk |

Specialist travel companies

So far we've concentrated on sites that provide a pretty general range of travel services. There are, however, a growing number of operators that cater for specific areas of the market such as student travel, late bookings and the over-50s.

If you're just looking for a family holiday or a business flight then you're almost certainly better off with the mainstream companies but, if you're looking for tailor-made travel, look no further.

Late bookings

Not only does the internet make it easier to get things done but it also makes it much quicker. As a result, a number of late booking sites have appeared, allowing you to arrange flights, holidays, weekend breaks and a whole world of other things – right up until the last minute. The mother of all late booking sites is Last Minute (www.lastminute.com) which still dominates the market but there are a few alternatives, mainly covering hotels and restaurants rather than how to get there. See the *Accommodation* section in Chapter 3 for more.

Last Minute www.lastminute.com

Specialising in impulse travel bookings rather than family package holidays, you'll find some rock-bottom prices on European travel and accommodation. If you're the sort of person who worries about every detail when making travel arrangements then you might not feel entirely comfortable with this type of service as there's not much time to confirm your booking. If, on the other hand, you love to live life on the edge and/or on the cheap – make sure you leave it to the Last Minute.

Sports and adventure holidays

For the ultimate holiday experience, it's hard to beat jumping off a crane tied to a piece of elastic, hurtling down a mountain on a plank of wood or crashing through the waves on a flimsy rubber raft. If bungee jumping, snowboarding or white water rafting sounds like your type of thing, there are plenty of travel operators who can provide your next adrenaline fix.

Board It www.boardit.com

Your one-stop shop for all things snowboardy. Make travel arrangements, find out the latest snowboarding news, browse the photo galleries and even check out a web cam of your chosen resort. A very well-put-together site which will appeal to beginners and pros alike.

1Ski www.1ski.co.uk

The sister site to Board It is equally impressive, offering travel booking, advice on skiing technique, stunning photography and everything else you need to go on the piste.

Maximise www.maximise.co.uk

If adventure sports are your thing, you'll be spoilt for choice here. Specialising in short breaks within the UK, Maximise offer a huge range of activities from paintball and karting to parachute jumping and white water rafting. If you see an activity break you like then you can book online, otherwise simply tell them what you want to do and they'll build a custom package for you. Regular adrenaline junkies may also want to check out the Maximise Club (**www. maximise.co.uk/club**) which offers some excellent discounts.

Adventure Directory **www.adventuredirectory.com**

No matter what activity you want to do (heli-skiing?) and where you want to do it (Wanaka?), a quick search through this massive directory of adventure sports providers will get you on the right track without delay. *Huuuuge.*

Young people and backpackers

If your idea of holiday heaven involves visiting strange places with your life on your back, you'll be spoilt for choice online. Any of the following companies will help you start your voyage of discovery but prices do vary so it's worth shopping around for the best deals. Once you've sorted out where you're going and how you're going to get there, flip forward to the *Accommodation* (p. 46) and *Travel* (p. 54) guides sections for more useful information.

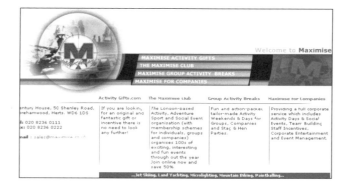

Trailfinders www.trailfinder.com

If you prefer something a little more exotic and you don't mind travelling without a tour rep then you'll definitely want to check out Trailfinders. The site may be a little sparse but there's more than enough to persuade you to ask for a brochure.

Campus Travel www.usitcampus.co.uk

Claiming to contain all you ever wanted to know about student and youth travel, this heavily discounted travel site is great for those in full-time education.

STA Travel www.statravel.co.uk

Already a firm favourite with students, STA Travel has created a suitably fresh and funky site which offers low-cost flights, overland travel and insurance services. You can make an online booking or use the site to find your nearest branch – there's over 250 to choose from.

Club 18-30 www.club18-30.co.uk

If you don't know about Club 18-30 holidays already, you probably wouldn't want to go on one. Sun, sea, sand and... so much more.

Senior citizens

In the early days of the internet, the average web surfer was about twelve years old and was only interested in music, chat rooms and the more, er, colourful side of the 'net. Nowadays the demographic make-up is much more representative of the real world and one generation in particular, the over-50s, is making some serious waves online. It comes as no surprise, then, that companies who traditionally target older people are realising the power of the internet to reach their customers. If you're over 50 and looking for a more relaxed holiday, why not try the following recommended sites.

Saga www.saga.co.uk

Synonymous with high-quality over-50s travel, Saga offer holidays to pretty much anywhere on the planet. They've also recently branched out into insurance and other financial services.

Vavo.com www.vavo.com

Although not strictly speaking a travel site, Vavo has a very useful travel forum and links directory aimed solely at the older holidaymaker. If you want to get away and Saga's not your cup of tea, you'll almost certainly find something suitable here. If you have no luck with the travel links, you can use the forum section to ask other users for their recommendations.

For more of the same see Active Lives (www.activelives.co.uk).

Flights

Most of the major airlines have very well-thought-out websites which allow you to check flight times, join frequent flyer schemes and, of course, book tickets.

There are some reasonably good discounts to be found but, with the exception of the low-cost services such as Go and Easyjet, you will rarely get the best fare when you book directly with an airline.

Low-cost airlines

Unlike their full-priced counterparts, the new breed of low-cost airlines offer some amazing fares to direct bookers. Most of the services offer more than acceptable standards of comfort and service so, if you're travelling within Europe and can survive without an in-flight meal, there really is no need to look anywhere else.

Once you've found your flight don't book it until you've compared prices with the other low-cost airlines – competition is fierce and there are huge savings to be made.

■ The best of the best

EasyJet **www.easyjet.co.uk**

It's orange, it's bold and it's excellent value. Easyjet, the web's favourite airline, offers low-cost flights a-plenty while taking every opportunity to have a dig at BA. Great stuff.

■ *The rest of the best*

Go www.go-fly

British Airways' low-cost offering has flights to a variety of European destinations. The service is ticket-less which means that once you've made your booking you can just turn up and, er, go.

Buzz www.buzzaway.com

British Midland may be a relative newcomer to the cheap flights arena but by allowing you to pay only for the extras you need they're on to a winner.

Virgin Express www.virginexpress.com

Virgin hop onto the cheap flight bandwagon with some very good deals between the UK and mainland Europe.

Full-fare airlines

The big boys of air travel have pumped plenty of money into their websites – and it shows. Flight arrival times, special offers, frequent flyer schemes and online booking make it easy to sort out your travel arrangements.

■ *The best of the best*

British Airways www.britishairways.co.uk

Realising the benefits of internet booking, especially for business travellers, British Airways have built a very impressive internet arm. Their main UK site offers online booking, special offers, flight times and everything else you could possibly need.

As is so often the case, a great site does not necessarily mean great prices and British Airways are noticeably more expensive than some of their competitors. However, if you're travelling on business and someone else is picking up the tab, BAs E-ticket service (which allows late booking and itinerary changes) will make travelling a breeze.

■ The rest of the best

British Midland www.britishmidland.co.uk

Like, BA, British Midland are certainly not the cheapest way to fly but you can save a few quid on the site's occasional ticket auctions. The site itself is one of the better-looking airline offerings, with flight times, booking information and more presented in a clear way.

■ The best of the rest

No matter which airline you choose, they'll almost certainly have their own website. Some have been slower than others to realise the potential of online booking so don't be surprised if you find little more than a glorified brochure on some of the smaller sites – keep checking back, they'll get there in the end. We hope.

Aer Lingus	www.aerlingus.ie
Aeroflot	www.aeroflot.org
Air Canada	www.aircanada.ca
Air France	www.airfrance.com
Air India	www.airindia.com
Air New Zealand	www.airnz.com
Alitalia	www.italiatour.com
American Airlines	www.americanair.com
Britannia	www.britanniaairways.com
Cathay Pacific	www.cathaypacific.com
Continental	www.flycontinental.com
Delta	www.delta-air.com
Eastern Airways	www.easternairways.com
El Al	www.elal.co.il
Finnair	www.finnair.co.uk
Iberia	www.iberia.com
Icelandair	www.icelandair.com
Jersey European	www.jea.co.uk
Kenya Airways	www.kenyaairways.co.uk

KLM	www.klmuk.com
Lufthansa	www.lufthansa.co.uk
Monarch	www.monarch-airlines.com
Pan Am	www.panam.org
Qantas	www.qantas.com.au
Ryanair	www.ryanair.ie
SAS	www.sas.se
Singapore Airlines	www.singaporeair.com
Swissair	www.swissair.ch
TWA	www.twa.com
United Airlines	www.ual.co.uk
Virgin Atlantic	www.virgin-atlantic.com

Airports

Before you travel it's well worth finding out a little more about where you're flying from. Most airport sites contain location maps, duty-free prices and general advertising blurb while some of the more internet-savvy operators provide real-time flight arrival information – very useful if you're arranging to meet someone off a particular plane.

■ The best of the best

A2B Airports www.a2bairports.com

The travel experts at A2B do it again with this indispensable guide to UK airports. Flight arrivals, how to get there and other useful nuggets of information make this a must for travellers and plane spotters alike.

The Complete UK and Ireland Airport Guide

A2bAirports.com features all the information you'll ever need when planning your trip: terminal guides, how-to-get-there maps and driving directions, contact telephone numbers for local taxi, bus, and train services, plus the latest flight arrival information (where available) and the very latest holiday departure price and availability details.

It's simple, just click on an airport name!

Scotland
Shetland Islands
Kirkwall
Aberdeen
Stornoway
Inverness
Edinburgh
Benbecula
Tiree
Glengedale
Campbeltown
Glasgow
Prestwick

Ireland
Belfast
Belfast City
Dublin
Cork

Isle of Man

The North
Newcastle
Teesside
Blackpool
Liverpool
Manchester
Humberside
Leeds/Bradford
Sheffield City

The Midlands
Birmingham
East Midlands
Norwich

■ *The rest of the best*

British Airports Authority **www.baa.co.uk**

Provides a gateway to some of the UK's largest airports, including Heathrow, Gatwick, Stanstead, Glasgow, Edinburgh, Aberdeen and Southampton. The most useful part of the site is the flight arrival information but there's also a photo gallery and some pretty gripping airport news.

London Luton **www.london-luton.co.uk**

Despite the fact that it's not actually *that* near to London (perhaps this is to confuse tourists), London Luton has become one of the busiest airports in the UK. The layout of their official site may be a little sparse but it's very well presented and contains all of the information you could possibly need, including real-time flight arrival information. Very nice indeed.

Manchester Airport www.manairport.co.uk

Claiming to be the gateway to the UK (aren't they all?), Manchester Airport has been on the web since 1996. The site contains the usual blend of passenger information, timetables and a list of duty-free shops – very useful for those who can't sleep until they know whether there's a Sock Shop in Terminal Two. There is.

■ The best of the rest

Birmingham International www.bhx.co.uk

Uncluttered site providing some useful information but nothing to write home about.

Exeter www.eclipse.co.uk/exeterair

'Connect to the world from Exeter'. Everything you ever wanted to know about the West Country airport.

Gloucestershire www.gloucestershireairport.co.uk

Surprisingly slick site with a wealth of useful information for and about those who fly there.

Isle of Man www.iom-airport.com

No-frills guide to Ronaldsway, the Isle of Man Airport.

Liverpool www.livairport.com

Check-in to the Merseyside base of British Midland, Easy Jet, Manx Airlines and Ryanair.

London City **www.londoncityairport.com**

Information about City Airport's regular flights to the heart of Europe.

Sea

Nautical travel may not be as well represented online as flying but the following sites should give you more than enough information to arrange your round-the-world trip or booze cruise to Calais.

Ferries

■ *The best of the best*

A2B Europe **www.a2beurope.com**

Another winner from the A2B stable. Provides information

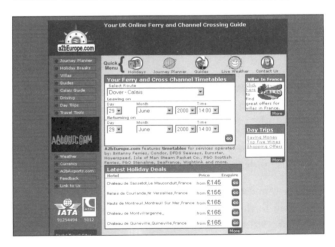

on ferries, hovercraft and more to help you cross the channel with ease.

■ The rest of the best

PTI Ferry Information www.pti.org.uk/docs/ferry.htm

Providing links to most of the UK's ferry operators. Be warned though, some sites are much better than others.

Ferry View www.seaview.co.uk/ferryview.html

A promising site which aims to become *the* independent ferry community on the 'net. Worth a look for its comprehensive list of links.

■ The best of the rest

Brittany Ferries www.brittany-ferries.com

Check sailing times, make an online booking or just ask for a free brochure. A very well-put-together site from one of the larger ferry operators.

Hoverspeed www.hoverspeed.co.uk

Hovercraft, Seacats and everything else that's not quite a ferry. A smooth site with plenty of added extras and a pretty adequate online booking facility.

Irish Ferries www.irishferries.ie

Ireland's leading ferry company (their words, not ours) have certainly put a lot of thought into their website. Internet booking, timetables and plenty of information to help you plan your journey.

P&O Ferries **www.poef.com**
Not content with just the one website, P&O have a whole family of the things. Choose the relevant one for a wealth of corporate, passenger and freight information.

P&O North Sea	www.ponsf.com
P&O Scottish	www.poscottishferries.co.uk
P&O Stena Line	www.posl.com

Red Funnel **www.redfunnel.co.uk**
Online booking, fare information and plenty of ferries with, er, red funnels.

Sea France **www.seafrance.co.uk**
The usual mix of secure booking, fares and timetables but with added fun for kids (and big kids) in the form of Cap'n Frank's fun and games.

Cruises

■ The best of the best
Cruise View **www.seaview.co.uk/cruiseview.html**
Fancy a holiday on the ocean waves but don't know where to start? Everything you ever wanted to know about cruises but were afraid to ask. See page 33 for web picture.

■ The rest of the best
Cunard **www.cunardline.com**
Sail into the sunset with the operators of the QE2 and other world-famous cruise liners.

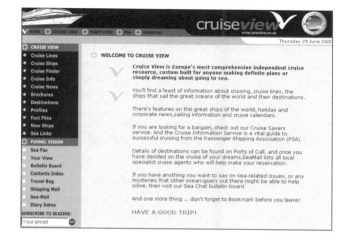

Boatastic www.boatastic.com

How they must have laughed when they came up with the name Boatastic. If you're the sort of person who actually knows which side is port and which is starboard this could well be the site for you. A massive range of boats and related products are available here at knock-down prices allowing you to have as many cruises as you like without a retired couple or sunset in sight.

The Royal Navy www.royal-navy.mod.uk

Can't afford a luxury cruise? Want a smart uniform? There's only one choice.

■ *The best of the rest*

Disney Cruises **www.disney.go.com/DisneyCruise**
Take to the seas with Mickey, Donald, Goofy and the rest of the Disney crew.

Swan Hellenic **www.swan-hellenic.co.uk**
Part of the P&O empire, Swan Hellenic offer cruises to Sweden, Russia, Estonia, Denmark, Norway, Scotland, Italy, Portugal and everywhere in between.

Thomson Cruising **www.thomson-holidays.com/cruises**
A little too much gushing over the joys of cruising and far too many clichéd 'sunset' photos but a pretty impressive site nonetheless.

Rail

Until quite recently, booking train tickets online was more hassle than it was worth, with most operators demanding that you use the telephone to book tickets. Nowadays, however, things are much rosier with the arrival of sites such as The Train Line and Eurostar's impressive offering. Once you've decided where you want to go you can find the quickest route at the best price and make an instant booking. Catching a train couldn't be easier – All aboard.

UK rail travel

■ *The best of the best*

The Train Line **www.thetrainline.com**
Save yourself the hassle of queuing at the station with this

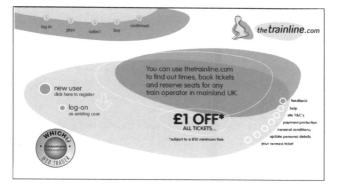

excellent site. Simply tell it where you want to go, what time you want to get there and what type of ticket you want. The site's booking system will check availability and allow you to book tickets instantly. For most journeys, the tickets will be sent to you by first-class mail but an increasing number of stations allow you to pick them up using an automated ticket machine. It's easy to use and works like a dream.

■ *The rest of the best*

Railtrack www.railtrack.co.uk

If you just want to check train times without actually booking tickets, Railtrack's searchable timetable is indispensable. Also contains network information and a nice mix of news and corporate blurb.

Eurostar www.eurostar.co.uk

Not strictly speaking a UK train operator but certainly one of the better rail sites. Includes an up-to-the-minute timetable, travel guides and online booking. Très bon.

Chester-Le-Track www.chester-le-track.com
Despite the site's slightly silly name (it's based in Chester-Le-Street, County Durham), it contains a comprehensive set of links to a wide range of UK transport information. From train booking to obscure trivia, it's all here.

UK Railways On The Net www.rail.co.uk
Not the most attractive site on the internet but it does contain a handy list of links to UK train company sites.

Orient Express Trains www.orient-expresstrains.com
Suitably classy site containing information about each of the Orient Express trains with a nicely presented photo gallery to give you an idea of what to expect. No sign of Poirot, though.

■ The rest of the best

Central Trains	www.centraltrains.co.uk
Gatwick Express	www.gatwickexpress.co.uk
Great Eastern	www.ger.co.uk
Great North Eastern	www.gner.co.uk
Great Western	www.great-western-trains.co.uk
Heathrow Express	www.heathrowexpress.co.uk
Northern Spirit	www.northern-spirit.co.uk
Scotrail	www.scotrail.co.uk
South West Trains	www.swtrains.co.uk
Virgin Trains	www.virgintrains.co.uk

European rail travel

Rail Europe **www.raileurope.co.uk**

If you're planning on travelling around Europe by rail, you'll probably want to save a few quid with a discount rail card. Also offers low-cost Interail cards for students.

Rail Connection **www.railconnection.com**

Another nice-looking site offering discounted European rail travel.

Road

Even though the internet was supposed bring the whole world straight to your desktop, there are still times when you need to hit the open road. Before you leave – don't forget to check out some of our recommended motoring sites which are guaranteed to make your journey that little bit smoother.

Motoring services

The major motoring organisations have tried very hard to become the driver's friend both in the real world and on the internet. The AA and RAC in particular have created superb motoring portals complete with automatic route calculators, travel news, hotel and restaurant reviews and pretty much everything else you need before you hit the road. If you're planning to join one of the larger organisations, look out for some quite good discounts if you sign up online.

■ *The best of the best*

The AA www.theaa.co.uk

Motoring heaven. This extremely well-thought-out site offers a very useful journey planner, traffic information and some excellent hotel and restaurant guides. The site is open to all, but AA members get exclusive access to a host of additional features and discounts. If you're not a member and are in the market for some breakdown cover, you won't be surprised to hear that you can sign up online.

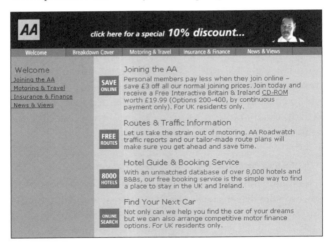

■ *The rest of the best*

The RAC www.rac.co.uk

Hot on the heels of the AA comes this impressive site from the RAC which offers a route planner, motoring advice, online membership and plenty more. Not quite up to the AA's standard but well worth a look, especially if you're already a member.

Green Flag www.greenflag.co.uk

It may not be as popular as the 'big two' motoring organisations but Green Flag have produced a site that's capable of mixing with the best of them. Here you'll find information about their range of breakdown services as well as a handy used-car checker.

Looking for directions? See Street maps in Chapter 3.

Car hire

Hiring a car online can be a confusing business. While most European car hire firms have realised the importance of having a separate UK site, some of their American counterparts are still relying on a UK page attached to their standard booking system. As a general rule, if you come across a site that doesn't know the difference between London, England and London, Canada – steer well clear.

■ The best of the best

BNM Airport Car Rental Guide www.bnm.com

Quite simply, if you want to rent a car from the airport you'll want to start here. Despite being based in America, BNM offers up-to-date car rental rates, booking information and more for pretty much every airport in the world. If you're not leaving the UK and don't want to travel to your nearest airport to pick up a car, try searching for 'Car rental' on Scoot (www.scoot.co.uk).

■ *The rest of the best*

If you need more information about a specific rental company or want to make an online booking, make sure you check out the following.

Easy Rentacar www.easyrentacar.com

Easyjet's spin-off car rental company allows you to choose a vehicle and book online. If you're renting a car in the UK, you'll find some great deals here.

Hertz www.hertz.co.uk

Hertz is one of the world's largest car rental companies so you'd expect something pretty impressive. Their online booking site is certainly one of the best in the business and their special offers make the deal that little bit sweeter.

■ *The best of the rest*

Avis www.avis.co.uk

Easy to navigate and complete with a secure system, it's hard to fault this site. Unless you don't like the colour red.

Budget www.budget.co.uk

Some good rental bargains to be had here if you can be bothered to trek through the online booking system. Fun but cluttered.

Europcar www.europcar.co.uk

More pictures of happy smiling drivers enjoying the experience of speeding in someone else's car. Guess what? Yup, you can make an online booking. Act surprised.

Kenning www.kenning.co.uk

If you think it's fun to rent a car – just wait until you get behind the wheel of a truck! Cross-channel alcohol shoppers rejoice.

National www.nationalcar-europe.com

National's European base has everything you'd expect from one of the larger vehicle rental names, including special sites for German, French, Italian and Spanish visitors. Nice touch.

Thrifty www.thrifty.co.uk

As well as allowing you to make rental arrangements this uncluttered site allows you to arrange long-term vehicle leasing and even buy a used car from a range which includes Fiats and BMWs.

U Drive **www.u-drive.co.uk**

U Drive – not just a name but also a definition.

Coach travel

Travelling by coach may conjure up images of school trips and WI outings but coach travel is still extremely popular. If you're travelling on a limited budget or going somewhere that is inaccessible by train, you could do a lot worse than checking out a few of the larger operators.

■ The best of the best

Go By Coach **www.gobycoach.com**

A nice move by National Express who have created a site which allows you to book their own services and also those

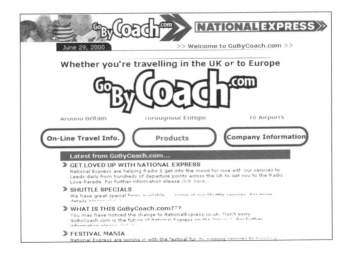

provided by the other companies they own. Almost all of Britain is covered and judging by the prices shown, they are certainly a much cheaper alternative to the train. The site itself doesn't disappoint either, with a very useful timetable and online booking system.

■ The rest of the best

Wallace Arnold www.wallacearnold.com

While other coach companies take care of the day-to-day business of getting from A to B, Wallace Arnold offer coach tours to a range of UK and European tourist attractions. A very well-put-together site which makes coach travel fun. Almost.

Busweb www.busweb.co.uk

A must-visit site for anyone with more than a passing interest in coaches and buses. Busweb contains links to most of the UK's operators as well as keeping you up to date with the very latest coach and bus news. Gripping stuff.

Public transport

It may be unreliable, dirty and expensive but Britain's public transport is used by millions of people each day. While the internet can't make things run any better, it can certainly relieve some of the stress by helping you to plan your journey in advance. Owing to the localised nature of public transport you won't find online booking services but if you need to find out what time the next bus is due and where it's going – you should find the information you need.

■ *The best of the best*

UK Public Transport **www.pti.org.uk**

This definitive guide to public transport in the UK provides instant access to a wealth of timetables, route plans, fares and much, much more. They're slowly improving the layout but UK Public Transport remains a superb example of content over style.

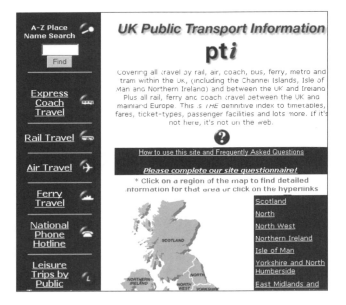

■ The rest of the best

London Transport **www.londontransport.co.uk**

Travelling around our nation's capital can be a stressful affair at the best of times. The official London Transport site has some very handy features, including a download-able underground map and a list of bus routes but, appropriately enough, it still needs a bit of work.

■ The best of the rest

Public transport operators have been amazingly slow to take advantage of the internet as a marketing and informa-tion tool, perhaps because many of them don't have to fight too hard for customers. Some of the larger companies are beginning to realise the benefits of going online so it's worth keeping an eye on the sites listed below. At least you can be safe in the knowledge that although you'll wait for ages for someone to create a decent site, two will probably come along at once.

Arriva	www.arriva.co.uk
Citylink	www.citylink.co.uk
First Group	www.firstgroup.com
Green Line	www.greenline.co.uk
Oxford Bus	www.oxfordbus.co.uk
Stagecoach	www.stagecoachholidings.com

3

places to go

Accommodation

Once you've picked your destination, your thoughts will probably turn to accommodation. Whether you're travelling on business in London or backpacking around Australia, the internet can help you find the best hospitality at the best rates – provided you know where to look.

If you're staying within the UK you can usually save money by booking directly with an established hotel chain or a small independent hotel rather than using a booking agent. It's a bit more risky booking directly with a foreign hotel so for added piece of mind you'll probably want to make your booking with either a travel agent or a reputable site like Expedia (**www.expedia.co.uk**) or Last Minute (**www.lastminue.com**). Regardless of how you choose to book, it's well worth checking your hotel out on the web before committing yourself.

For information on accommodation in the UK and around the world, check out our recommended sites.

Hotels

Although some prefer to rough it in a tent or share a crowded hostel room, most travellers will end up staying in one of the thousands of hotels around the world. Choosing the right accommodation can be almost as difficult as choosing your destination, with widely varying standards (four stars, five crowns, twelve olives?) and room rates. Fortunately, as you may have guessed, the internet makes it easier to find a bed for the night with plenty of websites offering information, ratings, pictures and even instant online booking facilities. The larger hotel groups usually have their own sites but if you want to get a better idea of what's available, it's a good idea to start with one of the main accommodation listing sites and work from there.

■ The best of the best

AA Hotel Finder www.theaa.co.uk/hotels

Over 8000 UK hotels listed and rated by the AA allowing you to choose accommodation with confidence. If nothing

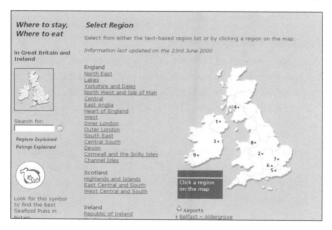

appeals, the RAC offer a similar service at www.rac.co.uk/services/hotelfinder.

■ *The rest of the best*

Leisure Planet www.leisureplanet.com

A massive resource containing photographs and information for over 50,000 hotels around the world. If you can't find something suitable here, you're probably too fussy to go on holiday anyway.

Places to Stay www.placestostay.com

Finding a hotel just got a whole lot easier. Places to Stay brings together a huge variety of international hotels with a very straightforward search system to find the one that best meets your requirements. This useful resource allows you to make an instant online booking and is an absolute godsend for business travellers.

Leisure Hunt www.leisurehunt.com

Another triumph of content over design. Search for a hotel or guesthouse anywhere in the world by location, price or facilities. The design is far from inspiring but the depth of information will certainly bring a smile to your face.

Infotel www.infotel.co.uk

Comprehensive database of UK hotels and guesthouses with location information, ratings and a booking system. Not the most easy to use site on the web but very useful nonetheless.

Late Rooms www.laterooms.com

If you're staying in the UK and have left things a bit late to arrange a hotel then you'll certainly want to check out the last-minute bargains available from Late Rooms. This well-laid-out site should have something that fits the bill but if you have no luck don't forget to try **www.lastminute.com**.

Holiday Rentals www.holiday-rentals.co.uk

Whether you're travelling in Scotland or St Lucia, this site will help you find your home from home.

Home Exchange www.homeexchange.com

Don't pay for a hotel abroad when you can just swap houses with someone who lives there. Plenty of houses, cottages and apartments on offer around the world.

■ *The best of the rest*

Forte www.forte-hotels.com

It's no surprise that one of the world's largest hotel chains has put together one of the most polished sites in its field. Find your nearest hotel from Forte's global portfolio in locations from London to Moscow.

Four Seasons www.fourseasons.com

'50 Hotels, 22 Countries, one Philosophy'. Wonderfully American in both style and sentiment.

Gleneagles www.gleneagles.com

If you're a golfer, you'll need no introduction to Gleneagles. If you're not, you'll probably want to look elsewhere. Worth visiting just for the stress-relieving screensaver and postcards.

Hilton www.hilton.co.uk

Fabulously trendy site full of short breaks, location information and plenty more. Includes the all-important online booking system which forces you to scroll through a huge list of locations rather than just letting you search. Ideal for visitors to the Aberdeen Hilton, not so good if you're headed to Zurich.

Intercontinental www.interconti.com

The information's all here but the site does appear to have been made entirely out of fuzzy felts.

Lanesborough www.lanesborough.com

You could argue that a hotel as famous as the Lanesborough doesn't need to bother advertising itself on the web. Still, the site contains all the information you need but there's plenty of room for improvement.

MacDonald www.macdonaldhotels.co.uk

In case the name hasn't given it away, MacDonald hotels are based in Scotland. Their great-looking site changes its design every season – a nice touch on a great site.

Mandarin Oriental www.mandarin-oriental.com

If you're heading to the Far East on business you definitely want to check out this pretty impressive site. There's even a slick video showcase to watch.

Marriott www.marriott.com

Another huge American site from another huge American hotel chain. If you're unlucky enough not to be staying in the US you'll have to put up with a much less attractive site – after all, it's your own fault.

Moat House Hotels www.moathousehotels.com

Stylish enough internet presence complete with details of the 40+ hotels that make up the UK arm of Queens Moat (www.queensmoat.com).

Novotel www.novotel.com

An appropriately uncluttered browsing experience awaits you at the official home of this comfortable but understated hotel chain.

Orient Express www.orient-expresshotels.com

The name itself conjures up images of a superior class of accommodation. You won't be disappointed.

Ritz www.theritzhotel.co.uk

It's the Ritz. It's in London. You know the rest.

Savoy Group www.savoy-group.co.uk

England's unashamedly upmarket hotel group have transferred all of their brand values onto this classy and informative site. We can't help but think that the special offers section may be wasted on many of the chain's more well-heeled guests.

Swallow www.swallowhotels.com

Online home of the UK hotel chain which has recently been, er, swallowed by Whitbread.

Thistle Hotels www.thistlehotels.com

If you've visited Thistle's site before but haven't been back for a while, you're in for a pleasant surprise. A recent facelift has transformed it into an extremely impressive affair complete with online booking and a WAP-enabled version.

Travelodge **www.travelodge.co.uk**

Weary travellers rejoice. Find a hotel, make a booking or just find your nearest Little Chef.

Hostels and Campsites

The accommodation of choice for students, backpackers and the cast of Carry-On films is surprisingly well represented on the web with most of the major hostels and campsites having their own website or at least being featured on someone else's. Hostels in particular are easy to find through a number of excellent online directories which allow you to search by location, facilities, price and more.

On the other hand, if it's a night under canvas you're after then look no further than the likes of UK Sites (**www.uk-sites.com**) and ABC Camping (**www.abccamping.com**). If you do have any problems finding something suitable, simply visit a search engine such as Google (**www.google.com**) and type in the name of the place you're looking for followed by the word 'campsite'.

■ The best of the best

Hostels.com **www.hostels.com**

Comprehensive independent listing of hostels around the world backed up with some very well-written advice for travellers. An absolute life-saver if you're travelling on a budget and need a bed for the night. Don't forget to print out the relevant listing for your destination before you travel – you'll be glad you did.

■ The rest of the best

Eurotrip **www.eurotrip.com**

As the name suggests, this is a resource for travellers around Europe. In addition to a useful (although far from complete) hostel listing, you'll find a range of articles, advice and links to help you on your way.

UK Sites **www.uk-sites.com**

The design and layout may leave a little to be desired but it's hard to fault the content. Over 2250 campsites are currently listed with more being added all the time. Simply choose a county for a full list of camp sites and caravan parks along with a contact phone number and postcode.

Hostelling International **www.yha.org.uk**

Representing over 4500 hostels in over 60 countries, this nice-looking site also allows you to apply for a discount card to save even more money.

ABC Camping **www.abccamping.com**

All the information you need to arrange a camping holiday in France. It's what all those school French lessons were for.

■ *The best of the rest*

The Traveller (Caravanning) **www.thetraveller.co.uk**

Leading the way for caravanning on the world wide web. Enough said.

UK Caravan Parks and Campsites **www.ukparks.com**

The British Holiday and Home Parks Association site allows you to find your nearest caravan park, camp site or chalet across the UK.

Travel guides

The internet is a great way to find out what to expect before you visit unfamiliar territory. Most countries, major cities and tourist attractions have their own official guide sites to help visitors get a feel for the place before leaving home and if you're travelling off the beaten track it can be well worth visiting one of the many Lonely Planet-type sites which allow you to swap advice and stories with your fellow adventurers.

World guides

If only Phileas Fogg had access to the internet before he started his journey around the world. Ok, so his adventures wouldn't have been half as much fun if he knew what lay around every corner and 'Around the World in 80 Clicks' doesn't have the same ring to it but if you're about to embark on an epic journey of your own, take a detour to a few of our recommended sites. Just don't forget to keep an eye on the time.

■ The best of the best

Fodors **www.fodors.com**
No matter where your holiday takes you, you'll want to start with a visit to Fodors. Covering the world's most popular

destinations, the site offers information on the best places to see, eat and stay along with well-researched advice for the first-time visitor. Also, if you want to buy a beer without shouting, make sure you visit the language centre to learn some essential phrases.

Beautifully written, well researched – this is one travel site you won't want to leave.

■ *The rest of the best*

Rough Guides travel.roughguides.com

A worthy contender to Fodors for the title of best backpacker travel site. Rough Guides have been kind enough to publish the entire contents of their books on the web, allowing you get a feel for the place you are going before you leave. Also, if all this travel information has fuelled your wanderlust, you can even book tickets and accommodation directly from the site. For the complete picture make sure you also check out the Lonely Planet site.

Lonely Planet Online www.lonelyplanet.co.uk

If you're planning on backpacking around the world you'll probably already own at least one of the Lonely Planet series. Here you'll find a wealth of information from their travel guides and an advice forum written by travellers around the world. Just remember to pop into a handy Tibetan or Egyptian internet café to add your own experiences to the board.

Virtual Tourist www.vtourist.com

Claiming to be 'the original travel community', Virtual Tourist is definitely a strong contender for the title, having been around since 1994. Over the years the site has grown from being a simple world guide to something of a travel monster with over 31,000 destinations covered in amazing detail. The real beauty of the site is the fact that much of its content is written by members in the form of discussion boards and travel pages, allowing you to get a feel for a place from someone who's already been there.

World Travel Guide www.wtgonline.com

Another site that started off as a book – this time it's Columbus Publishing's World Travel Guide that gets the digital treatment. Not quite up to the standard of Lonely Planet or Rough Guide but if you're looking for a brief, well-written guide to the world's cities and countries you'll find it (and more) here. There's even a German version if you're feeling fluent.

National Geographic www.nationalgeographic.com

A whole world of information for the more adventurous traveller. Maps, forums, interactive features and, of course, plenty of award-winning photography make this site worth visiting even if you have no intention of travelling outside Cheltenham.

The Hitchhikers Guide to the Galaxy www.h2g2.com

There can't be many sites that can claim to be a travel guide for the entire galaxy but, then again, there aren't many authors like Douglas Adams. The Hitchhiker's Guide is like a tourist information site for alien visitors and attempts to explain everything there is to know about earth and beyond from the sensible ('All about Brussels, Belgium') to the bizarre ('Train Station Psychosis'). A word of warning: if you plan to visit this huge site during your lunch break, don't expect to do any more work for the rest of the day. As addictive as it is brilliant.

■ The best of the rest

The Discovery Channel **www.discoverychannel.com**
Travelling? Do it like they do on the Discovery Channel.

Travellers Bookstore **www.travellersbookstore.co.uk**
Rough guides, maps and plenty of other reading material for holidaymakers and travellers.

Wish You Were Here...? **www.wishyouwerehere.com**
Judith Chalmers and her happy band of celebrity holiday chums welcome you to their (very tanned) world.

Country guides

Arctic explorers will be please to hear that even Greenland has its own website (**www.greenland-guide.dk**) providing a wealth of useful information for visitors to one of the most chilly, yet awe-inspiring, countries on earth. Don't worry if you're headed for warmer climates – every country in the world has some kind of internet presence, either an official tourist information site or a less official 'things to do in...' type of affair. As ever, we've tried to bring together the best and most popular sites but if your destination of choice is missing, simply refer to the World guides section for the necessary information.

■ *The best of the best*

At UK www.atuk.co.uk

If your travel ambitions stretch only as far as the UK, this is most definitely the site for you. Every county is featured with details of accommodation, tourist attractions and even a range of live web cams so you can see where you're going before you get there. Splendid.

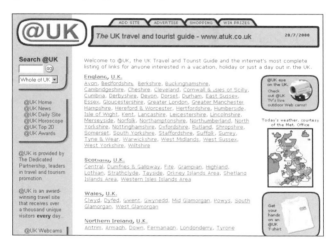

■ *The rest of the best*

Africa Guide www.africaguide.com

It's interesting that one of the least developed countries in the world should have one of the best tourist websites – perhaps countries like Austria and the USA don't have to work as hard to attract visitors? Africa Guide provides a wealth of advice for visitors and is also used as a means to attract foreign aid and charity donations. An easy-to-navigate front page makes it a simple matter to find the information you need and, if you're planning to visit, it'll tell you all you need to know.

Greenland www.greenland-guide.dk

It may be one of the coldest places on the planet but Greenland has produced a surprisingly hot website to promote its wildlife and, er, ice. For the adventurous there's plenty of information about dog sledding and whale watching while animal lovers will be captivated by the pictures of furry creatures. If you're not a big fan of frostbite you may not want to actually visit Greenland but if you want a holiday that is guaranteed to be free of screaming children, this could be your idea of heaven.

■ The best of the rest

Australia www.australia.com

Take a virtual trip to the home of koalas, kangaroos, barbecues and Rolf Harris. Strewth.

Austria www.austria-tourism.at

Official tourist guide to the wonders of Vienna, Salzburg, Innsbruck and plenty of mountains.

Belgium www.visitbelgium.com

The plucky Belgians are clearly trying to persuade visitors that good things come in small packages by describing themselves as 'a country the size of Maryland'. It certainly convinced us.

Brazil www.brazilinfo.com/index_en.htm

A complete Brazilian portal including a hotel directory, tourist information, an impressive photo gallery and some very useful statistics and maps.

Carribean www.caribtourism.com

If you're planning a totally tropical trip you'll find plenty here to whet your appetite. There are individual guides to each of the islands, a calendar of events, video footage and you can even send off for a free vacation planner.

Denmark www.visitdenmark.com

Just when you thought Denmark was only about bacon. Up-to-date news, travel tips and plenty of photos of young trendy Scandinavians.

Egypt www.touregypt.net

Official site from the Ministry of Tourism that will have you walking and talking like an Egyptian in next to no time.

France www.francetourism.com

They may be our nearest European neighbours but if your knowledge of all things French stops at 'la plume de ma tante' you'll want to spend some time on this information-rich site.

Germany www.deutschland-tourismus.de/e/

Everything you ever wanted to know about Germany but were too lazy to ask. A very busy site filled with forthcoming events, weather forecasts, gushing tourist blurb and an interactive slideshow. Wunderbar.

Greece www.travel-greece.com

It may have become the destination of choice for clubbers and party animals but, as this site proves, Greece also has more than enough to satisfy even the most laid-back traveller.

Ireland www.ireland.travel.ie

It may be closer to home but Ireland is more than capable of competing with more distant holiday locations. Accommodation, places of interest, festivals, news and more shamrocks than you could shake a stick at.

Italy www.italiantourism.com

Pizza, pasta, wine and there's even some culture mixed in for good measure.

Japan www.jnto.go.jp

An insight into the people, the culture, the design and, yes, even the raw fish.

Netherlands www.holland.com

Canals, tulips, diamonds, Van Gogh and some very popular cafés. Be sure to check out the straight-talking Smart Guides.

Portugal www.portugal.org

An incredibly hip-looking official site from the Portuguese Tourist Board complete with links to other useful information sites and resources.

Russia www.russia-travel.com

Discover the magic of Russia without freezing to death in

the process. The site is quite basic but the information's there if you dig deep enough.

Switzerland **www.switzerlandtourism.ch**

You already know about the secret bank accounts, chocolate, clocks and James Bond films which have made Switzerland famous – now find out the rest.

USA **www.usatourist.com**

Links to each of the states, links to the many tourist attractions, a currency converter and a man in a silly hat. God Bless America.

Place guides

It's hard enough deciding which country you want to go to, but once you get there how can you make sure you see as much as possible without investing in a million guide books? From theme parks to entire cities, anywhere that gets its fair share of tourist traffic will probably have a website and there's no better place to start than our guide to the best of the bunch.

■ *The best of the best*

Time Out **www.timeout.com**

London's Living Guide goes global with a wide range of fresh and funky guides to the world's cities. If you're planning a family holiday with the kids, this may not be the site for you. If, however, you want to party in Prague or chill-out in Chicago, there really is only one choice.

■ *The rest of the best*

Wcities www.wcities.com

It's no surprise that some of the best city guides tend to be written by people who actually live there – Wcities being no exception. Local writers in over 30 countries provide constantly updated advice for business and leisure travellers and the information is even available on WAP-enabled mobile phones and handheld computers.

London www.londontown.com

If you're planning a trip to our nation's capital – or just want to be reminded about how much there is to do there – you'll want to check out the official London tourist site. Reviews of clubs, restaurants, theatre and fashion give a great overview of the city while the events diary will be as useful to locals as it is to tourists.

Paris www.paris.org

Split into three sections – the city, culture and tourist information, this is certainly one of the better city guide sites on the web. Whether you're planning a visit to the Eiffel tower and want to know what time it opens or you just want to find out more about the romance capital of Europe, you'll find all the answers within easy reach. When it comes to Paris, if it's not here – it's not worth knowing.

New York www.nyctourist.com

New York – home of the Empire State Building, the Statue of Liberty, Yellow Cabs, *Ghostbusters II* ... the list goes on and on. The official site of the city that never sleeps contains plenty of information about what to see, where to go and, perhaps most importantly, how to stay safe. There doesn't seem to be much missing but if you do have any questions, you can always ask Joe the Doorman.

If you want to have a proper look around New York before you decide whether to make the trip, why not take a virtual tour with Strolling (www.strolling.com).

Great Barrier Reef www.great-barrier-reef.com

Although nothing can prepare you for the amazing beauty of the Great Barrier Reef, the official site is essential viewing before you go. Not only does it provide all of the information you need to plan your holiday but you can also take advantage of its nifty booking system to book accommodation and arrange some diving lessons.

Disney World www.disneyworld.com

This suitably cute official site is filled with information about the world's most famous theme park all wrapped up in pictures of smiling children and, or course, That mouse. Fun and games a-plenty ensure that younger visitors will fall under the Disney spell while the day planner and online ticket booking make it easy for grown-ups to succumb to pester power. Just don't forget to wish upon a star.

Amsterdam www.channels.nl

Although not the most polished site on the web, a lot of effort has gone into putting together this virtual tour of Amsterdam's most famous areas. After you've clicked your way around the city, you can check out some of the local restaurants, hotels and tourist attractions and, if you fancy seeing Amsterdam in real life, you can even book online.

Beach Beats www.beachbeats.com

If your idea of holiday heaven is a fortnight in the clubs and bars of Ibiza or Ayia Napa, this site was designed for you. Alongside club guides and features from the likes of Kiss100 and Mixmag there's weather information, travel tips and some excellent travel bargains. Smooth.

Thorpe Park www.thorpepark.co.uk

As one of the UK's leading theme parks, you'd expect Thorpe Park to have a pretty impressive website. Fortunately the home of the Tidal Wave doesn't disappoint with a virtual guide to the park, information about the latest rides and even online ticket booking to plan your visit in advance. White-knuckle fans should also check out Chessington World of Adventures (www.chessington.co.uk) and Alton Towers (www.alton-towers.com).

■ The best of the rest

Disneyland (Paris) www.disneylandparis.com
Disney's European outpost is colourful, exciting, informative and so very, very Disney.

Disneyworld (Florida) www.disney.co.uk/usa-resorts/wdw
The Florida one. It's all here – the parks, the accommodation and, of course, the characters.

Edinburgh www.edinburghguide.com
An extremely well-put-together directory of places, events and news for the Scottish capital. Achieves the difficult goal of appealing equally to tourists and locals.

Niagara Falls www.niagara-usa.com
No frills to be found here, just plenty of pictures and paragraphs of gushing (pun intended) tourist information.

The Solar System www.nasa.gov
Ok, so it's unlikely that you'll be taking a holiday to the Moon or Mars just yet but when the time comes you'll be glad that you've done your research. Check out the amazing photographic archive full of pictures taken by astronauts and satellites.

Maps

Finding your way around unfamiliar cities is difficult enough but finding your bearings in a foreign country takes real skill – and a good map. As luck would have it, the internet is packed full of suitably decent maps for almost every street, town, city or country you might find yourself in. Just don't forget to print them out before you leave.

Street maps

There's nothing worse than travelling halfway across the world only to get lost trying to find your hotel. Luckily help is at hand in the form of sites such as Multimap (www.multimap.com) in the UK and Mapquest (www.mapquest.com) for the rest of the world which allow you to view detailed street maps simply by typing in a postcode, street name or region.

■ The best of the best

Multimap **www.multimap.com**

No matter how good your sense of direction is, it helps to have a decent map. Multimap is much more than decent as

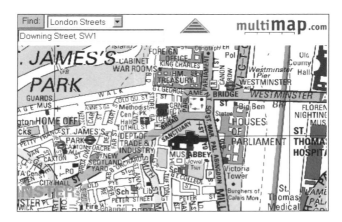

it allows you to enter any UK postcode or street name and instantly see a detailed map of the area. It's tools like this that make the internet worthwhile.

■ The rest of the best

Mapquest www.mapquest.com

Map Quest can be summed up in one word – huge. The main feature of the site is its map database which will display a street map for pretty much any area in the world. If you want one you can take with you in the car, you can either print it out or order it from their well-stocked shop.

Expedia Maps www.expedia.co.uk/daily/resources

If Map Quest doesn't fit the bill, Expedia also allows you to search for maps for any major city or area in the world. The level of detail is not quite as good as Multimap but when you've got this level of coverage it's difficult to complain. As a nice bonus, each map also comes with links to useful local information.

Maps.com www.maps.com

If quality and detail are important to you, you'll probably need to spend some money on a proper map rather than using a service like Multimap or Map Quest. Maps.com allows you to buy maps in either downloadable digital format or on paper. Even if you're not in a buying mood there's still plenty to see here, including an education section and nicely put together list of links.

Atlases

Whether you're planning a world tour or arguing over which continent Russia's in there's no disputing the fact that atlases can be pretty useful. Again, it only takes a quick surf around the web to get the bigger picture – as the following recommended sites more than ably demonstrate.

■ The best of the best

Atlapedia www.atlapedia.com

The world is constantly changing and, more often than not, traditional maps are out of date the moment they're printed. If you want to keep track of changes in place names, borders and politics, you'll need a site like Atlapedia. Offering an array of colourful maps backed up with geographic, economic and cultural information, this site is a must for globe trotters and geography students. See page 71 for web picture.

■ The rest of the best

Terraserver www.terraserver.com

Not strictly a map site but well worth a look – if only for the novelty value. Features aerial photos of places of varying importance around the world, including major tourist attractions and airports. Hours of fun for Russian spies and lazy plane spotters.

Travel advice

Although we've already dealt with travel guides for particular countries (see World guides, p. 55 and Country guides p. 58) there are plenty of sites offering more general advice for first-

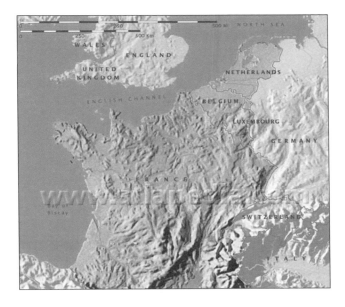

time and experienced travellers alike. Travel advice sites generally fall into one of two categories: useful or life-saving. The useful sites aim to make your trip more enjoyable whereas the life-saving ones are there to make sure you get home in one piece.

General travel advice

No doubt your Auntie Maureen's tips for getting a decent cup of tea in Rhyl go down a storm at the local WI but if it's genuinely useful travel tips you crave, you'll find everything you need on the web. From keeping safe when travelling alone to making the most of your gap year, you can be sure that someone who's been there and done it will be happy to pass on their pearls of wisdom.

■ The best of the best

About Travel **home.about.com/travel**

Although the vast majority of the information here is aimed at an American audience, the site's sheer depth means that you're bound to find what you're looking for if you dig deep enough. About.com uses real people to suggest appropriate links to appropriate information on everything from travel vaccines to treasure hunting. If you

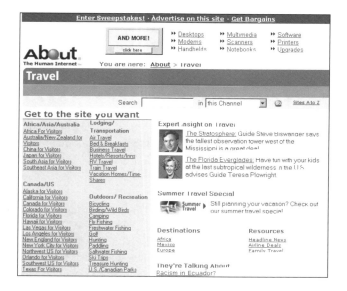

can't find the right section try searching fron
menu page at **www.about.com**.

■ *The rest of the best*

Tips 4 Trips **www.tips4trips.com**
A forum for travellers to exchange tips and advice. The
quality of the advice varies wildly, a particular favourite
being 'Make sure you won't be vacationing in land
mines...on toxic beaches', but overall the contributors seem
to know what they are talking about. Also offers a Tip 4 The
Day e-mail newsletter.

Epicurious Travel **travel.epicurious.com**
From the publishers of *Traveller Magazine*, Epicurious
Travel offers the usual mix of travel information and tips.
The best part has got to be their world events guide which
will make sure that you never miss the party.

Outside Online **www.outsidemag.com**
Fans of the great outdoors will love this award-winning
magazine dedicated to adventure and adventurers. Tales of
courage and endurance are mixed with advice and discussion, making this an enjoyable destination, for the more
active traveller.

The Backpackers Guide **www.backpackers.net**
Invaluable for both first-time and more experienced backpackers, The Backpackers Guide offers some excellent
advice to ensure a trouble-free summer break or gap year.
Written in a friendly style by people who have clearly been

out there and done it, this site provides all you need to begin your Littlest Hobo-esque adventure.

The Complete Gap Year www.gapyear.co.uk

So you've finished your exams and the choice is whether to spend your gap year seeing the world or stocking shelves in Tesco. If you want to take the former route then a trip to The Complete Gap Year is absolutely essential – otherwise it's off to www.tesco.com.

Excite Travel www.excite.com/travel

If Excite Travel wasn't so American you probably wouldn't need too many other travel sites. Essentially just a handy directory of travel-related sites, you'll find links to every-thing from American Express to the Weather Channel.

Art of Travel www.artoftravel.com

Intelligent advice for travellers on a budget – clearly written by someone who's travelled the world and learnt the hard way.

Health and legal advice

If you restrict your travels to UK soil then you shouldn't encounter any problems more serious than a burst tyre or a nasty wasp sting. If, however, you've set your sights slightly further afield, there's plenty of information on the web to keep you safe, well and on the right track.

■ *The best of the best*

Centre for Disease Control and Prevention www.cdc.gov/travel

User-friendly health advice for British travellers. Provides warnings about health risk areas, disease prevention advice

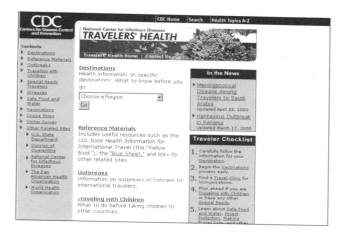

and links to other useful resources. Although this is the government's official guide site, if you are worried about staying healthy when travelling it is worth visiting some of the other health sites for more in-depth information.

■ The rest of the best

Foreign and Commonwealth Office www.fco.gov.uk

Avoid getting caught up in a military coup or malaria epidemic by consulting the government's Foreign and Commonwealth Office before you travel. The advice is usually up to date but you'll still need to be careful when visiting volatile areas.

Embassy Web www.embpage.org

This complete list of embassies covers almost every nationality in almost every country and will prove invaluable if you find yourself in trouble abroad. Unfortunately the site doesn't include the dates of the Ambassador's receptions so you'll have to buy your own Ferrero Rocher. *Excellente*.

Travel Health www.travelhealth.com

A very useful site which claims to be the premier health resource for travellers. While there are a few other health sites who would argue with their claim, you would be hard pushed to find broader coverage of health and safety risks for people on the move. Travel Health is operated by an American travel medicine store so make sure you shop around before buying anything on the site.

Travel Safety Tips www.travelsafetytips.com

Concise yet potentially life-saving advice for travellers. If it doesn't make you more careful it'll certainly make you paranoid.

UK Passport Agency www.ukpa.gov.uk

Of course you'll have no need for this site as you've checked that your passport is valid, right? If for any reason you need to get hold of a passport application kit in a hurry or would just like to find out how to take the perfect passport photo (we kid you not), the answers are here.

Travel insurance

Although travel agents would probably like you to believe otherwise, you don't have to buy your travel insurance from the same place as you booked your holiday. If you don't want the hassle of making your own arrangements then most of the larger online travel bookers will be able to organise travel insurance on your behalf but, as an internet booker, you have the advantage of being able to shop around for the best cover without having to leave the house. To get a good idea of what you should expect to pay, your first stop should be a rate comparison site like the rather nifty Screentrade (www.screentrade.co.uk) which allows you to compare prices from the UK's leading insurers. If you want to do your own price checking then you'll find direct links to the most popular companies at Find (www.find.co.uk/ insurance). Once you have made a shortlist of your options, you can visit the individual insurer's websites to find out exactly what cover is provided and, having made a final decision, some services will even allow you to sign up online. For the full low-down on insurance and other money matters, check out Zingin's, *The very best money websites.*

■ *The best of the best*

Screentrade www.screentrade.co.uk

If you want to find the best value travel insurance on the web you can either waste hours trawling through the thousands of policies available or, alternatively, spend ten minutes letting Screentrade do the searching for you. Basically, you type in details of the type of cover you're looking for and the site will compare prices from the leading UK insurance companies to find the best deal for you – even allowing you to sign up online using a credit or debit card. Simple but very effective.

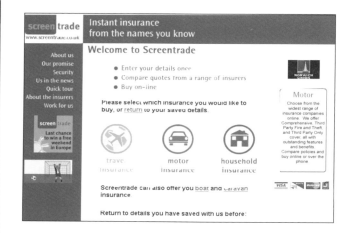

■ *The rest of the best*

Columbus Direct **www.columbusdirect.net**

How travel insurance should be done. Simply tell them a
few details about who you are and where you're going and
Columbus will provide an instant quote and even allow you
to sign up online. The prices are usually very competitive
and Columbus have been in the business long enough to
know the type of cover that travellers need.

Rapid Insure **www.rapidinsure.co.uk**

Rapid Insure have obviously decided that insurance websites aren't cool enough and have set out to produce a
suitably funky alternative. Behind the gloss though, it is
surprisingly easy to sign up to the cover you need. The site
claims that you can arrange a policy in just three clicks and,
unlike many of its competitors, you actually can. Simply tell

them what type of cover you need (click), decide on the package that best suits you (click) and confirm your order (click). The policies are designed to meet your holiday requirements and there's plenty of information to help you decide what's right for you. An insurance site that's nice looking and useful too – who'd have thought it?

Find www.find.co.uk/insurance

The focus of Find is clearly to provide an up-to-date directory of links to UK insurance websites rather than wasting time on flashy design and moving pictures. If you want to make sure that you've checked out all of your options before taking out a policy, make sure you've found Find.

Travel Insurance Club www.travelinsuranceclub.co.uk

A no-frills site outlining the Travel Insurance Club's award-winning range of policies for backpackers and winter sports enthusiasts. At the time of writing, there's no facility to book online but the relevant contact details are there so it's easy enough to arrange cover.

■ *The best of the rest*

Direct Travel www.direct-travel.co.uk

Functional insurance site complete with online booking and details of their award-winning policies.

Quote Wizard www.quotewizard.co.uk

Let the Quote Wizard wave his magic wand and conjure up some pretty competitive travel cover.

Sore Eyes **www.soreeyes.co.uk**

A constantly updated guide to online insurance companies. If you're looking for a brief run-down of your options, it's well worth taking a look here.

4

useful tools and information

The reason many people travel abroad is to experience something different – different languages, different weather, different currencies, different everything. While it's exciting to learn about a country as you travel, you can give yourself a head start (while avoiding jetlag, sunstroke and poverty) with some of the web's most essential information sites.

Language

We British have a great tradition of shouting and waving our arms at waiters and shopkeepers when travelling abroad rather than learning the language. If, however, your basic conversational French or Hungarian is not up to scratch you might want to take a crash course with one of our recommended sites.

■ *The best of the best*

Travelang **www.travlang.com**

This no-frills site is a great first stop for learning the basics of a foreign language. Once you've chosen where you're travelling to, you are presented with a list of useful phrases which may not make you fluent but will certainly allow you to get by without resorting to mime. For more complex translations, check out Travelang's online dictionaries at **dictionaries.travlang.com**.

■ *The rest of the best*

Fodors Language **www.fodors.com/language**

One of the best sites for learning basic conversational French, German, Italian or Spanish. Fodors are already renowned for their excellent travel guide site and this invaluable resource is the icing on the cake.

Babel Fish world.altavista.com

Fans of *The Hitchhikers Guide to the Galaxy* will recognise the Babel Fish as a translating fish which caused more wars than anything since the history of creation. On the internet, however, Babel Fish is actually a very nifty translation tool from AltaVista. As an added bonus, why not try converting English to French and then back again for an amusing one-player game of Chinese whispers. Literally minutes of fun.

BBC Education (Languages) www.bbc.co.uk/education/languages

Spanish, French, German, Italian and Welsh are all covered on this multimedia resource from the BBC. Rather than trying to be a standalone language course, the site ties in with the BBC's Learning Zone and visitors are encouraged to combine internet learning with TV programmes and other material. Having said that, even if you don't fancy staying up late to watch the programmes there's still more than enough here to get you started, including specially produced audio and video learning aids.

Linguaphone www.linguaphone.co.uk

If you want to go the whole hog and learn a language properly, you'll need a proper in-depth course – and who better to provide it than Linguaphone? You'll have to shell out some pretty serious cash to start learning but it's money worth spent if you travel regularly.

Currency

Even with the advent of the single European currency it's still inevitable that you're going to need to change your hard-earned money into something more suitable. Before visiting your friendly local bureau de change it's a good idea to cast your eye over one of the many currency sites which provide up-to-the-minute exchange rates, ensuring that you get the most for your money.

■ *The best of the best*

Oanda **www.oanda.com**

There's a huge amount of foreign exchange information to be found here. If your interest in the world's currencies goes beyond finding out how much French wine you can get for your pound you'll be spoilt for choice with news, up-to-

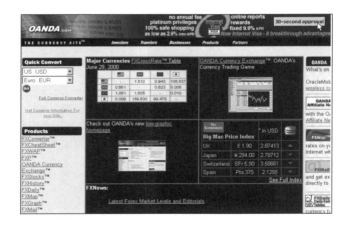

the-minute rate information and even a currency trading game. Don't even bother with other exchange sites until you've been here.

■ The rest of the best

Yahoo! Foreign Exchange uk.finance.yahoo.com/forex.html

Quick and easy to use, Yahoo!'s foreign exchange tool does the job with the minimum of fuss. Simply tell it how much of which currency you need to change and click the convert button. Splendid.

Universal Currency Converter www.xe.net/ucc/

Although the UCC contains fewer features than Yahoo!'s offering, it's perfect if you're just looking for a quick foreign currency conversion. Simple but very effective.

Travelang Currency www.travlang.com/money

Another useful service for the popular Travelang site. Not only can you convert between most of the world's currencies but you can also track their exchange rate history to see how much you could have got if you'd planned in advance.

Mastercard ATM Finder www.mastercard.com/atm

Possibly the most useful of all the useless tools on the web. Next time you need to withdraw some money, simply pop along to your nearest internet café or fire up your laptop (which you always have with you, right?) and find your nearest cash machine. To be fair, if you have access to the web from your mobile phone it's pretty useful but for most people its main use is to waste some time checking that your favourite hole in the wall is listed. Trust us, it will be – they all are.

American Express Travellers Cheques www.americanexpress.co.uk

Avoid carrying around large amounts of money while you're travelling. Simply tell them where you are and AmEx will point you in the direction of their nearest foreign exchange or travellers' cheque agent.

Western Union www.westernunion.com

Running out of money needn't mean the end of your holiday. Western Union's global site allows you to arrange a money transfer and find your nearest agent anywhere in the world.

Time

Now, thanks to the power of the internet, you can make your jetlag even worse by comparing local time with the time back home. Great.

■ *The best of the best*

Time and Date www.timeanddate.com/worldclock

Find out what time it is anywhere in the world – all on one page. One of those tools that doesn't look like much but that you'll visit time and time again. Great stuff. See page 87 for web picture.

■ *The rest of the best*

World Time Zone www.worldtimezone.com

A bit more complicated than Time and Date, with world time

⊙www.timeanddate.com

| Menu: | Main Page | Time Zones | World Clock | Calendar |

The World Clock

[Full List] [Options] [**Search**] [Meeting Planner] [Fixed Time]
[Africa] [North America] [South America] [Europe] [Asia] [Australasia]
[**Personal World Clock**] [Sort by Country] [Sort by Time]

Current local times around the world (Standard version)

Addis Ababa	17:18	Geneva *	16:18	New Orleans *	09:18
Adelaide	23:48	Guatemala	08:18	New York *	10:18
Aden	17:18	Halifax *	11:18	Oslo *	16:18
Aklavik *	08:18	Hanoi	21:18	Ottawa *	10:18
Algiers	15:18	Harare	16:18	Paris *	16:18
Amman *	17:18	Havana *	10:18	Perth	22:18
Amsterdam *	16:18	Helsinki *	17:18	Phoenix	07:18
Anadyr *	03:18+	Hong Kong	22:18	Prague *	16:18
Anchorage *	06:18	Honolulu	04:18	Rangoon	20:48
Ankara *	17:18	Houston *	09:18	Reykjavik	14:18
Antananarivo	17:18	Indianapolis	09:18	Rio de Janeiro	11:18
Asuncion	10:18	Islamabad	19:18	Riyadh	17:18

zones displayed on a colourful map which somehow manages to make it seem much more confusing. Great for geography students but a bit too much like hard work for the rest of us.

Weather

Holiday brochures are usually full of pictures of fantastic weather and sun-soaked beaches with not so much as a dark cloud in the sky so it's always a little annoying when you arrive in the middle of the monsoon season without having packed a pair of wellies. If you want to contest your travel agent's climatic claims, our recommended sites will allow you to moan with absolute accuracy.

■ *The best of the best*

The Met Office **www.met-office.gov.uk**

A stylish site from those bright and breezy folk at the Met Office. Not satisfied with providing up-to-the-minute weather forecasts, they also give you access to satellite pictures, charts and climate information. Some official government sites can give you the impression that they've been thrown together in an afternoon but it's obvious that the Met Office have gone out of their way to provide information in a clear yet comprehensive format. Outlook: Bright.

■ *The rest of the best*

The Weather Underground **www.wunderground.com**

Continually updated forecasts and temperature information for the entire planet make this a great place to get a
quick overview of the world's weather.

Despite the site's sinister-sounding name it's not actually
the headquarters of a group of renegade weathermen
determined to overthrow the Met Office's evil meteorologi-
cal dictatorship. At least we don't think it is.

Yahoo! Weather **weather.yahoo.com**

Yahoo! proves once again that it is the traveller's friend with
this handy round-up of the world's weather. Being an
American site, the emphasis is on the weather in Memphis
rather than Manchester but you'll find most cities in most
countries covered.

Keeping in touch

Even once you've arrived at your destination the internet
has plenty to offer. From free e-mail to cheap telephone
calls it's never been easier to communicate – after all, that's
what the net was built for. Also, while you're away, don't forget to pop into a local internet café to send an e-postcard to
the folks back home.

E-mail

Free web-based e-mail has spread like wildfire amongst
people on the move. If you are never in the same place long
enough to collect your messages, services like Hotmail
(**www.hotmail.com**) will give you a free e-mail account which

can be accessed from any internet-connected computer in the world. It's important to look around before signing up to a web-based service as many of the established services have a huge number of users, making it difficult to get the address you want. Hotmail and Yahoo! Mail (mail.yahoo.com), for example, each have millions of members and so addresses like john@hotmail.com or sarah@yahoo.com were taken years ago. If you want a memorable name then it's a good idea to look at some of the lesser-known services or those that offer thousands of different addresses, such as Another (www.another.com).

■ *The best of the best*

Another www.another.com
If you want a free e-mail address that reflects your personality, you'll love the range offered by Another.com. After

you've chosen your free address from the likes of **you@babe-magnet.co.uk** or **you@thedigerati.co.uk** you'll be able to send and receive messages from anywhere in the world. The huge list of available addresses means that you're bound to find something that sums you up.

■ The rest of the best

Genie **www.genie.co.uk**

You'll never be worried about missing a message again with this nifty free e-mail service from Genie. Simply sign up for a free e-mail address and you'll be notified via your mobile phone every time a new message arrives. If that's not enough to satisfy your hunger for information, there's plenty of other useful stuff to be had, including news headlines and sports results. Functional and free – 'nuff said.

Hotmail **www.hotmail.com**

The mother of free e-mail services, Hotmail allows you to sign up for a free e-mail account which can be accessed from any online computer in the world. The only downside is that millions of addresses are already taken so unless you are happy to be **a_very_long_name33@hotmail.com**, you might want to look elsewhere.

■ The best of the rest

Purple Turtle **www.purpleturtle.com**

UK-based, feature-packed e-mail service which promises to give 20% of its advertising revenue to help turtle conservation around the world. It's worth supporting them for their charitable contributions but the service is pretty good too!

Yahoo! Mail mail.yahoo.com

Yahoo! may have been the original search engine but they're still playing catch-up with the long-established Hotmail service.

Postcards

Although most e-mail postcards are far too cute for anyone except for ten-year-old American girls, they can be useful when travelling in a country with an unreliable postal system. Although the types of cards and methods of delivery vary from site to site, the general principle is that you choose your card, personalise it with a message (wish you were here, perhaps?) and send it to as many recipients as you wish. Be warned though, it's very easy for them to send one back to you, thus starting an almost unbreakable chain of sending them a postcard to thank them for your postcard thanking them for their postcard... and so on.

■ The best of the best

Blue Mountain www.bluemountain.com

Avoid the cost of stamps and postal delays by sending your postcards by e-mail. Blue Mountain is the busiest postcard and greetings site on the web, offering a massive selection of free cards which are guaranteed to arrive home before you do. See page 93 for web picture.

■ *The rest of the best*

E Greetings **www.egreetings.com**

Thoroughly American greeting cards to let people know you're thinking of them. Avoid being overcome by some of the more sentimental cards by laughing yourself silly at gems like 'Happy National Hotdog Month'.

Hallmark **www.hallmark.com**

This nice-looking site from the king of high street card shops offers some pretty funny cards in addition to the usual range of gooey sentiment. Well worth a look if Blue Mountain and E Greetings make you feel nauseous.

Keekaboo **www.keekaboo.com**

Electronic postcards are fun if you're on a tight budget or too lazy to write but there is no substitute for the real thing.

Keekaboo allows you to send a real postcard, delivered by a real postman, anywhere in the word – free of charge. The service is supported by advertising so don't expect a huge choice of cards but when you're getting it all free – who cares?

Telephone

There's no getting away from it – international phone calls are expensive. The advent of internet telephony (making calls over the net) promises to bring costs down but until the technology is perfected and sufficiently widespread you'll still need to pour loose change into phone boxes or endure huge mobile phone bills.

There are, however, a few sites that can make it easier (and sometimes a bit cheaper) to keep in touch with the folks back home.

■ The best of the best

Contact Box www.contactbox.com

Billing itself as 'The all in one messaging solution', Contact Box should prove very useful if you want to keep in touch while you're travelling. After signing up to the free service, you are given a personal Contact Box telephone number which will forward your calls to almost any other phone in the world. If you're not going to be near a phone or you just want to get away from it all, Contact Box will even record a message and send it to you by e-mail. When you get home, you'll have hours of fun exploring the other free Contact Box services, including web space, reminders, chat rooms, web cards and much more. See page 95 for web picture.

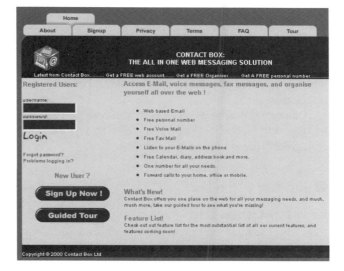

CONTACT BOX:
THE ALL IN ONE WEB MESSAGING SOLUTION

Latest from Contact Box......... Get a FREE web account....... Get a FREE Organiser........ Get A FREE personal number.........

Registered Users:

username:

password:

Login

Forgot password?
Problems logging in?

New User ?

Sign Up Now !

Guided Tour

Access E-Mail, voice messages, fax messages, and organise yourself all over the web !

- Web based Email
- Free personal number
- Free Voice Mail
- Free Fax Mail
- Listen to your E-Mails on the phone
- Free Calendar, diary, address book and more.
- One number for all your needs.
- Forward calls to your home, office or mobile.

What's New!
Contact Box offers you one place on the web for all your messaging needs, and much, much more, take our guided tour to see what you're missing!

Feature List!
Check out our feature list for the most substantial list of all our current features, and features coming soon!

Copyright © 2000 Contact Box Ltd

■ The rest of the best

International Dialling Codes **www.whitepages.com.au/wp/time.shtml**
Simply type in the name of the country you're calling from and where you're trying to call and in seconds you'll have the correct code. There's not really much more to say except that it works perfectly and it'll even tell you the correct local time.

YAC **www.yac.com**
While not offering the same range of features as Contact Box, YAC does have some very nice call-handling features which will appeal to those who want a bit more control over their messaging.

Internet cafés

Just because you're away from home doesn't mean you can't get online to check e-mails, find tourist information or just surf the web. Internet cafés have spread like wildfire and whether you're in Aberdeen or Africa, you're bound to find one nearby.

Although the range of services vary in each café you will usually find access to the web, printing facilities and enough caffeine to keep you awake for hours.

■ The best of the best

Net Cafes www.netcafes.com

Net Cafes' exhaustive list includes price information, directions and a list of the services offered by each café. Just

don't forget to print out the relevant list before you go otherwise it rather defeats the object.

■ The rest of the best

Easy Everything **www.easyeverything.com**
Although not much use if you're backpacking around Australia, Easy Everything offer some of the best-value web surfing in the UK. Find your nearest location, get the latest news and information or even apply for a job on this predictably orange site.

Clothing and luggage

Seasoned travellers know just how important it is to make sure you have the right clothes and equipment before setting off. Luckily the internet can help you find everything from sandals to scuba gear – often at very competitive prices.

We've suggested a range of sites which offer the best service and value for money but also make sure you visit shop directories like 2020shops (**www.2020shops.com**) which will allow you to check your options before you part with your hard-earned cash.

Clothing and accessories

Although the number of online clothing retailers continues to grow, the simple fact is that clothes are one of the hardest things to buy over the web. No matter how hard they try, internet traders cannot allow you to try on a pair of shoes or a shirt before you buy. What they can (and usually do) offer, however, is a decent returns policy so that if the cap doesn't fit – you don't have to wear it.

Before buying it's important to find out what you can do if you buy the wrong size, colour or style and, more importantly, how much you'll be charged for returning items. To be fair, most clothing e-tailers will offer a free, no-quibble returns policy but there are still a few who will refuse to refund or replace purchases. This is especially true of swimwear and shoes so make sure you ask before you buy.

■ The best of the best

Blacks **www.blacks.co.uk**

Lovers of the great outdoors rejoice! Blacks offer a complete range of hiking shoes, rucksacks and related outdoor

wear. The prices may not be the cheapest in the business but the site looks great and products can be ordered online (with free delivery) or picked up from your nearest high street branch.

■ The rest of the best

Legends Surf Shops www.legends-surf-shops.co.uk

If your idea of fun is standing on a plank of wood and getting wet, cold or bruised then you'll certainly want to surf over to Legends. All types of boards are featured here, including surfboards and snowboards, and if you're feeling creative you can even build your own skateboard. Nice.

Complete Outdoors www.complete-outdoors.co.uk

The name says it all. Shoes, bags, tents, walking poles and everything else you might need to get back to nature. The prices are pretty down to earth too, although you will have to pay extra for postage.

Board Riders www.boardriders.co.uk

If the name hasn't given you a pretty good idea what this site is all about, it's probably not for you. Snowboards, surfboards, wind surfing and all the kit that goes with it. The prices are competitive but if you really want to splash out (pun intended), interest-free credit is available.

Discount Sports www.discountsports.co.uk

No matter whether you're seriously sporty or just want to keep cool abroad, Discount Sports will have something to suit you. Trainers, T-shirts and other sportswear with free delivery and – you've guessed it – discounted prices. If you're not happy with a purchase, they'll send you a refund (minus postage) in the form of a credit note.

Newitts www.newitts.co.uk

Although mainly a sports retailer, Newitts stock a limited but fashionable range of men's and women's swimwear. If you're expecting an active holiday, you'll also find shoes, clothing and even trampolines.

■ The best of the rest

Explorers Online www.explorers-online.com

Swiss Army knives, Ordinance survey maps, navigation tools and everything else you need to make it safely to the shops and back.

Redoute www.redoute.co.uk

Swimwear and much more besides from the UK home of French fashion and style.

Luggage and essentials

■ The best of the best

Luggage Line www.luggage-line.com

A whole world of luggage awaits you at this very nicely designed site which offers free delivery and excellent customer service. The prices are pretty competitive too.

■ *The rest of the best*

Boots www.boots.co.uk

Keep yourself safe on holiday with a complete range of sun-care products and first aid kits. In addition to the shopping, there's also a forum, health and beauty advice and Advantage Card holders can earn points while they shop. A high street retailer that knows how to work the web – whatever next?

Simply Scuba www.simplyscuba.co.uk

Another self-explanatory name. Offers a wide range of diving equipment and all the clothing that goes with it.

Luggage Express www.luggage-express.co.uk

BAA's chosen online luggage retailer offers a decent range of hand luggage, suitcases and bags on wheels. The prices

are pretty good but it's worth shopping around for a better deal.

Condomania www.condomania.co.uk

If you're expecting a romantic holiday, you'll want to stock up here before travelling. There's a wide range to choose from and all orders are dispatched in a plain wrapper to avoid knowing looks from the postman. Stop sniggering at the back.

Travellers Bookstore www.travellersbookstore.co.uk

Unless you've got a laptop computer with plenty of battery life you'll either have to print out a whole load of stuff from the online travel guides or buy yourself a real paper-based guidebook. Travellers Bookstore offer a large range of guidebooks which you either buy on their own or as part of a package tailored to your chosen destination. The prices quoted on the site are all below the publisher's recommended price but if you know which title you want you'll probably getter a better deal from one of the larger online bookstores such as Amazon (www.amazon.co.uk) or BOL (www.uk.bol.com).

Fun stuff

As you've probably noticed, not everything on the internet is entirely useful – in fact some of it is just plain weird. The following sites can be safely ignored if you're planning a business trip but if you fancy a laugh, they make essential viewing.

■ The best of the best

Airtoons www.airtoons.com

Flight information cards may not be a natural source of comedy but that didn't stop the creator of airtoons seeing the funny side. Comedy genius.

■ The rest of the best

Earth Cam www.earthcam.com

See the world from the comfort of your computer with this huge collection of live cameras around the world. From Big Ben to the Bahamas – it's all here.

In the event of an aircraft evacuation, style points will be given according to style and artistic impression.

Dialectizer www.rinkworks.com/dialect

If you're fed up with translating from English to French and German why not try something different? A particular favourite is the English to Elmer Fudd translation – absolute poetry.

■ The best of the rest

Bikini.com www.bikini.com

An American (where else) site dedicated to all things Bikini. The creators claim that the site is aimed at women but with games like 'dress the model' it probably receives more than its fair share of male visitors. There's not much to it but it looks great – a bit like bikinis really.

Find a Grave www.findagrave.com

Laughing in the face of good taste, this slightly morbid site allows you to track down the final resting place of your favourite (ex) celebrity. Great if you're fed up with traditional tourist attractions and want to do some alternative sight seeing.

Tube Hell www.tubehell.com

As anyone who regularly travels on it regularly will testify, there's plenty of room for improvement on the London Underground. However, the commuters are fighting back, using the power of the internet. Tube Hell is a site dedicated to complaining about how unreliable, dirty and just plain bad the service is, with stories of nightmare journeys aplenty. If you're one of London's thousands of tube sardines – this one's for you!

Pylon of the Month **www.pylonofthemonth.com**
Ok, so you're on a tight travel budget and fascinated by science – why not combine both your hobbies and become a pylon spotter? For a fine example of pylon perfection to get you started, check out Pylon of the Month.

Air Sickness Bags **www.airsicknessbags.com**
A site dedicated to rediscovering your lunch. Enough said.

Information on the move (WAP)

The internet is great if you happen to be within easy reach of a computer. Although internet cafés have become extremely widespread it can still be a bit of a chore trying to find one in an unfamiliar city, especially if you only want to confirm your travel arrangements or check the weather forecast for your next port of call. The answer, of course, is Wireless Application Protocol or WAP, which allows you to view the internet (or at least a cut-down version of it) on your mobile phone.

If you want the full blown multimedia experience of the web then you're still going to have to rely on an internet café or laptop but if you can cope with no-frills browsing, grab your mobile phone and check out a few of our favourite WAP sites.

Please note: The following sites are only accessible from WAP-enabled phones.

■ The best of the best

Google wap.google.com

Already our search engine of choice, Google was the first search engine to really 'get' WAP. Not only can you access their entire database of sites (not just the WAP ones) but if you click on a link to a non-WAP link, Google will translate the page for viewing on your mobile. Bringing the entire web to your mobile phone – another masterstroke.

■ The rest of the best

Wcities www.wcities.com

Wcities' website is already a great tool for travellers but the service really comes into its own when you access it on your mobile phone. Information and advice for the world's cities delivered straight into the palm of your hand anywhere in the world. It's great and it works.

The AA www.theaa.co.uk

The AA is making very good use of WAP technology with a genuinely useful set of tools for motorists. As you'd expect, all of the latest travel and route information is available but the real gem is the traffic news service which will let you search for delays and accidents simply by typing in the name of the road you're travelling on. A simple tool which works exactly as it should.

Thomas Cook wap.thomascook.com

An entire high street travel store on your mobile phone. Although at the time of writing there was no facility to book via WAP, you'll find the latest travel offers, contact information and plenty more besides. Also check out E Bookers (**wap.ebookers.com**).

Last Minute **mobile.lastminute.com/wap**

Considering that the whole point of Last Minute is to allow you to make spontaneous travel arrangements, you probably won't be surprised that they have made WAP a major part of their development plans. A superb WAP effort which is perfect if you want to arrange a flight while standing in the middle of a field.

My WAP World **www.mywapworld.com**

Mobile phones have always been great for arranging to meet friends and generally planning your social life but with the arrival of WAP you can access a wealth of other information without leaving the party. Want to find out where your favourite DJ is playing or just looking for cheap beer? Look no further.

Still looking?

Although we've tried to cover the most useful and interesting online travel resources we're not infallible (hard to believe but true!).

If you can't find the information you're looking for then why not visit us on the web? The Zingin Travel Guide (**www.zingin.com/guide/info/travel**) contains all of the sites listed here plus an up-to-date directory of the best new resources for travellers and holidaymakers.

Don't panic if you're still having no luck, just surf over to our Search Guide (**www.zingin.com/guide/search**) where our team of human search experts will try their hardest to help you out – and it won't cost you a penny!

quick reference guide

Low-cost airlines 23

Full-fare airlines 24

Airports 27

Coach travel 42

Public transport 43

Hotels 46

Hostels and campsites 52

World guides 55

Maps 67

Atlases 70

General travel advice 71

Fun stuff 102

WAP 105

Zingin links